Plant Cycle

Published in the United States of America by Cherry Lake Publishing
Ann Arbor, Michigan
www.cherrylakepublishing.com

Reading Adviser: Marla Conn MS, Ed., Literacy specialist, Read-Ability, Inc.
Content Adviser: Brittany Burchard M.Ed., Science teacher
Book Design: Jennifer Wahi
Illustrator: Jeff Bane

Photo Credits: © lovelyday12 / Shutterstock.com, 5; © Rawpixel.com / Shutterstock.com, 7, 23; © TinnaPong / Shutterstock.com, 9; © Brocreative / Shutterstock.com, 11; © Elizaveta Galitckaia / Shutterstock.com, 13; © Vinin / Shutterstock.com, 15; © Amelia Fox / Shutterstock.com, 17; © Michelangeloop / Shutterstock.com, 19; © Elena Yakusheva / Shutterstock.com, 21; Cover, 2, 3, 6, 12, 20, 24, Jeff Bane

Library of Congress Cataloging-in-Publication Data

Names: Bell, Samantha, author. | Bane, Jeff, 1957- illustrator.
Title: Plant cycle / by Samantha Bell ; [illustrator, Jeff Bane].
Description: Ann Arbor, MI : Cherry Lake Publishing, [2018] | Series: My
  world of science | Audience: K to grade 3.
Identifiers: LCCN 2017030507| ISBN 9781534107243 (hardcover) | ISBN
  9781534108233 (pbk.) | ISBN 9781534109223 (pdf) | ISBN 9781534120211
  (hosted ebook)
Subjects: LCSH: Plant life cycles--Juvenile literature. | Growth
  (Plants)--Juvenile literature.
Classification: LCC QK49 .B36 2018 | DDC 581--dc23
LC record available at https://lccn.loc.gov/2017030507

Printed in the United States of America
Corporate Graphics

About the author: Samantha Bell has written and illustrated over 60 books for children. She lives in South Carolina with her family and pets.

About the illustrator: Jeff Bane and his two business partners own a studio along the American River in Folsom, California, home of the 1849 Gold Rush. When Jeff's not sketching or illustrating for clients, he's either swimming or kayaking in the river to relax.

Most plants start as seeds.

The seed needs soil. It needs
water. It needs sunlight.

The seed **sprouts**. Leaves and roots start to grow. Now it is a seedling. It has a stem.

The seedling grows. It becomes a **mature** plant.

Buds grow on the plant.
The buds **bloom** and become
a flower.

When do you see flowers blooming?

The flowers make more seeds.

Some seeds fall on the ground.

Other seeds are spread around. Some are very light. They can blow in the wind.

Some seeds float. They move with the water.

Some seeds are sticky. They stick to clothes. They stick to fur. People and animals carry them to new places.

What kinds of seeds have you seen?

Some flowers become fruit.
They might be strawberries.
They might be apples.

New seeds are inside or outside
of the fruit.

Some **scientists** study plants.
They ask questions. They look
for answers.

What would you like to study next?

glossary

bloom (BLOOM) to produce flowers

mature (muh-CHOOR) fully grown

scientists (SYE-uhn-tists) people who study nature and the world we live in

sprouts (SPROUTS) begins to grow and produce branches or buds

index